AdEx---(ADX)
Advertising exchange.

Aeternity---(AE)
Decentralized apps (Prototype)

Ardor----(ARDR)
Blockchain for spawning blockchains.

Ark----(ARK)
Blockchain switchboard.

ALT Coins---(ALT)
A digital currency other than Bitcoin.

ATMChain---(ATM)
Advertising network.

Augur----(REP)
Decentralized prediction market.

Bancor-(BNT)
Token Index Funds.

Basic Attention-(BAT)
Decentralized Ad Network.

Binance Coins-(BNB)
Coin where you pay Binance exchange fees.

Bitcoin- (BTC)
Digital Gold

BitcoinDark-(BTCD)
Zcoin close.

Bitdeal-(BDL)
Bitcoin clone.

Bitquence-(BQX)
Mint for cryptocurrency investments.

BitShares-(BTS)
Decentralized exchange.

Blackout- (BM)

When Bitcoin or a alt-coin decreases in value and holders or people that know of coin freak out.

Blocknet-(BLOCK)
Decentralized exchange.

Bubble-(Bub)
A negative phrase people use that don't fully understand Bitcoin. This word can also be used on other crypto's. This word is also used when people think Bitcoin or an alt-coin is a scam.

Byteball Bytes-(GBYTE)
Decentralized database and currency.

Bytecoin-(BCN)
Privacy-focused cryptocurrency.

Bytom-(BTM)
Physical assets as tokens.

BITCOIN DICTIONARY

(...C...)

ChainLink- (LINK)
External data for contracts.

Civic- (CVC)
Identity and Authentication App.

Coinpot- (COINPOT)
A online site that lets you hold and earn Bitcoin and other crypto for free. They have a small fee for certain wallets.

Coin Market Cap-
(no abbreviation)
A crypto version of the stock market. You can sell , buy and thousands of crypto that exist all over the world.

Great to see the top 100 crypto.

Cryptocurrency-(crypto)

a digital currency in which encryption techniques are used to regulate the generation of units of currency and verify the transfer of funds, operating independently of a central bank.

"decentralized cryptocurrencies such as bitcoin now provide an outlet for personal wealth that is beyond restriction and confiscation"

Cryptonex-(CNX)

Zerocoin clone.

CPU-(CPU)

A battery.
CPU can be used to mine crypto or Bitcoin. Phones , Computers and Antminer/Crypto miners have a

strong CPU to mine Bitcoin. It's never good to mine with a weak battery as it earns less and can crash your device.

CPU Speed-(no abbreviation)

The set speed for battery of device to mine. The common mining process speeds are: Low CPU usage, Medium CPU usage and High CPU usage.

Decred-(DCR)

Bitcoin with alternative governance.

DigiByte-(DGB)
Faster Bitcoin.

Digital Cash-(DC)
Money that may be transferred electronically from one party to another during a transaction.

DigixDAO-(DGD)
Organization that manages tokenized gold.

Dogecoin-(DOGE)
A coin once made a popular meme joke but took off serious as millions adopted the penny coin. This coin is used as a joke coin among high coin traders. Don't worry I believe in the doggy.

Doggeycoin- A word typically said when mispronouncing dogecoin. Dogecoin fans also sometimes purposely use this phrase to honor the dog in the coin's image.

Dashcoin- A peer-to-peer cryptocurrency that was forked out of Bitcoin to offer faster and more private transactions to users. **Dash** is the first digital **currency** with a decentralized blockchain governance system. **Dash** is a blendword for Digital Cash and its **currency** symbol in the markets is **DASH**

Edgeless -(EDG)
Decentralized casino

Ethereum -(ETH)
Programmable contracts and money.

Electroneum-(ETN)
Monero clone.

Ethereum Classic-(ETC)
Ethereum clone.

Electroneum-(ETN)
is a brand new British cryptocurrency Developed to be used in the mobile gaming and online gambling markets, it will be the most user-friendly cryptocurrency in the world with-- --

--wallet management and coin mining all possible on a mobile app.

Electricity-(no abbreviation)
A form of energy resulting from the existence of charged particles (such as electrons or protons), either statically as an accumulation of charge or dynamically as a current.

FairCoin-(FAIR)
Bitcoin that rewards savers.

Factom-(FCT)

Decentralized record keeping.

FunFair-(FUN)
Decentralized casino.

{ ...G... }

GameCredits-(GAME)
Video game currency.

Gas-(GAS)
Pay fees on Neo.

Gnosis-(GNO)
Decentralized prediction market.

Golem--(GNT)
Rent other people's computers. Typically used for online mining purposes. Sometimes when you do cloud mining you're renting sometimes hash or computer power.

GXShares-(GXS)
Decentralized Chinese Equifax.

(...H...)

Hash- (HASH)
A number of mining speed. Example; Current hash rate: 0 H/s, 5 H/s. A good hash is 10 for a low CPU device such as a phone and 100 or more for stronger devices such as computers or Antminers. You can make millions if your device goes above 900 H/s

Hashtag- (HT)
A nickname for Hash.

Hash mining- (HM)
Where you mine crypto and see a H/s.

HShare- (HSR)
Blockchain switchboard.

ICO-(ICO)

An unregulated means by which funds are raised for a new cryptocurrency venture.

In an **ICO** campaign, a percentage of the cryptocurrency is sold to early backers of the project in exchange for legal tender or other cryptocurrencies, but usually for Bitcoin. Most ICO's tend to be scams wanting your Bitcoin or Fiat though some are good if you know when to pull out.

ICO scams are a large reason why people call Bitcoin and all crypto's a 'bubble'.

Iconomi -(ICN)
Digital asset investment funds.

IOTA -(MIOTA)
Internet-of-things payments.

[...]...)

Komodo-(KMD)
Decentralized ICOs

KuCoin Shares-(KCS)
Profit-sharing exchange investments.

Kyber Network-(KNC)
Decentralized exchange.

Litecoin-(LTC)
Faster Bitcoin.
Well it's not technically 'Bitcoin' but it has a nickname as the second Bitcoin as it was the second cryptocurrency made after Bitcoin.

Loopring-(LRC)
Decentralized exchange

Lykke-(LKK)
Digital asset exchange.

Lisk -(LSK)
Decentralized applications in JavaScript.

MaidSafeCoin-(MAID)
Rent disk space.

MCAP-(MCAP)
Mining investment fund.

MonaCoin-(MONA)
Japanese Dogecoin.

Metal-(MTL)
Payments with rewards program.

Metaverse ETP-(ETP)
Chinese Ethereum plus identity.

Monaco-(MCO)
Cryptocurrency credit card.

Monero-(XMR)
Private Digital Cash.
This currency is very fast to mine on your phone.

NAV Coin-(NAV)
Bitcoin with private transactions.

Neblio-(NEBL)
Decentralized application platform.

NEM-(XEM)
Batteries-included digital assets.

NEO-(NEO)
Chinese-market Ethereum.

Nexus-(NXS)
Bitcoin clone.

Nxt-(NXT)
Cryptocurrency and marketplace.

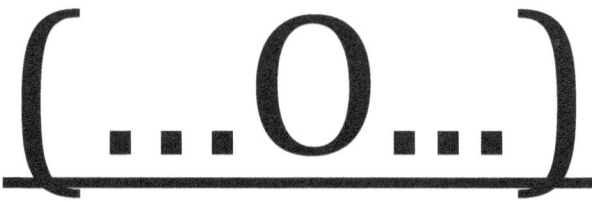

Open Trading-(OTN)
Decentralized exchange.

0x--- (ZRX)
Decentralized exchange.

Particl-(PART)
Privacy marketplace and chat.

Pura-(PURA)
Cryprocurrency.

PIVX-(PIVX)
Inflationary Dash clone.

Populous-(PPT)
Invoice trading futures.

Power Ledger-(PORW)

Airbnb for electricity.
Typically used to mine on someone else's electricity.

https://techcrunch.com/2017/11/19/100-cryptocurrencies-described-in-4-words-or-less/

www.ingramcontent.com/pod-product-compliance
Lightning Source LLC
Chambersburg PA
CBHW030600220526
45463CB00007B/3127